D0603155

DISCOVER
NORTHLAND

DISCOVER NORTHLAND

PHOTOGRAPHS BY WARREN JACOBS

TEXT BY NEVA CLARKE McKENNA

KOWHAI
PUBLISHING LTD

Published in 1993 by
Kowhai Publishing Ltd
10 Peacock Street, Auckland.
1051 Dyers Pass Road,
Governors Bay, Christchurch.
Photographs: Copyright
© Warren Jacobs Photography Ltd
Text: Copyright
© Neva Clarke McKenna

Reproduction of the whole or any
part of the contents without written
permission is prohibited.

Design: Warren Jacobs
Artwork: John Burt Graphics, Christchurch
Typesetting: TypeShop, Christchurch
Printed in Hong Kong
ISBN 0 908598 58 0

Endpaper:
Bay of Islands, Aerial

Page 2:
Pahi Bay, Northland

Department of Survey and Land Information
Map Licence 1993/101:
Crown Copyright Reserved.

Cape Reinga

Spirit Bay

Cape Maria van Diemen

Te Pak

INTRODUCTION

Justifiably Northland is known as the cradle of New Zealand's history. According to legend, it was in Doubtless Bay on the east coast that the first Maori, Kupe, set foot, and from Hokianga on the west coast that he left to return to his homeland. Later Maori found the climate inviting, the bush-covered hills supplied wood for canoes and birdlife for food, the soil was suitable for growing kumara, the sea provided a plentiful fish supply, while the succulent pipi, tuatua and toheroa lay buried in the sand.

Abel Tasman, the first known European to sight New Zealand, named Cape Maria van Diemen and the Three Kings Islands. As Captain Cook was sailing past the North Cape in 1769, the French Jean Francois Marie de Surville was anchored in Doubtless Bay. Before long whalers from all over the world began to take an interest in the Bay of Islands in particular, trading nails, blankets, beads and even muskets for food and water. Their loose living made life difficult for missionaries of the Catholic and Wesleyan faiths and those from the Church Missionary Society. The British Admiralty's awareness in the 1830s of the use it could make of the magnificent kauri tree and New Zealand flax saw the province's first two industries develop.

Immigrants began to arrive from England and elsewhere in the 1850s, travelling to their unseen land by what was then the highway—the sea. Surnames of those on the shipping lists of the day remain throughout Northland.

The province stretches for more than 400 kilometres from Auckland to Cape Reinga. Driving winds blowing across the Tasman combine with tumultuous seas to form huge sand dunes, bringing a spectacular and awesome grandeur to the western shoreline. Washed by the gentler Pacific Ocean, the east coast is less rugged but no less exciting, with its scalloped beaches and comparatively undisturbed waters. At Cape Reinga the two oceans meet and appear to quarrel, an intriguing sight. Throughout Northland today sheep, cattle and deer farms and vineyards and orchards are interspersed with patches of native bush and extensive pine plantations. In some areas the landscape is dotted with volcanic cones, while pa sites on hillsides are reminders of Maori occupation of yesteryear. Northland's only city, Whangarei, has a population of around 40,000 and it is here that most light and heavy industry is based. However, forestry and tourism are fast developing from north to south, while signs direct travellers to cottage industries of variety and quality—to glass-makers and painters, wood turners and artists, spinners and weavers, furniture makers and potters. In the harbours fishing fleets sit alongside yachts and other pleasure craft, some owned privately, others by tourist operators.

Northland's sub-tropical climate and lengthy coastline make it a magnet to those who enjoy being close to sea, in the sea, on the sea, or under the sea. It is also where visitors can see sub-tropical fruit and shrubs and flowers, where they can visit a glowworm grotto, thermal pools with healing properties, see magnificent forests and waterfalls, take gentle or strenuous walks on the mainland and also on islands. Other gifts of the area are its clean air, its breathtaking sunsets and its remoteness, all of which are rapidly being discovered by holiday-makers. Those who live in Northland have always known these treasures were theirs.

Because of its architecture, the old Custom House (left) in Russell is often mistaken for an early church. Of heart kauri, it was built in 1879 as the residence and office of the Collector of Customs. It also housed the post office. Today it is the town's police station. The magnificent tree on the roadway immediately in front of it is a Moreton Bay Fig. The tree trunk and the building are two of Russell's most photographed subjects.

7

Cape Reinga lighthouse (left) stands in grand isolation. Through the roots of a pohutukawa tree at the foot of the rocky headland the spirit of the Maori is said to descend on its return to its homeland in Hawaiiki. The first lighthouse in the area was built on nearby Motuopao Island in 1879. On its transfer in 1941 to Cape Reinga (Te Rerengawairua or Place of Leaping) the light was converted into an automatic battery unit and since 1987 has been fully automatic. Controlled electronically, the light flashes every 26 seconds and can be seen for 50 kilometres. Named by Abel Tasman in January 1643 in honour of the wife of the governor of the Dutch East Indies, the nearby Cape Maria van Diemen (top above) is the habitat of the flax snail (*Placostylus*). Once abundant, its numbers have been sadly depleted by wild pigs so that an area is now reserved for the protection of those which still survive. The pohutukawa or Christmas Tree (above), grows extensively throughout Northland, especially along the coastline where it often clings to rock faces. In the flowering season trees along the foreshore drop a carpet of red on to the sand below. Pohutukawas (*Metrosideros excelsa*) provide welcome shade for holiday-makers, and children make great use of their widely spreading branches.

Everyone should do the bus trip to Cape Reinga once in a lifetime. Depending on tides, buses travel one way by road, the other along the incomparable and magnificent Ninety Mile Beach (bottom right) which is, in fact, slightly less than 90 kilometres in length. There are enjoyable stops along the way and lunch is often a smorgasbord at a pleasant spot. Buses travel part of the way along the bed of the Te Paki Stream bed (above right) where there is an opportunity of climbing enormous sandhills. The patterns in the sand are constantly changing as the direction and severity of the wind alter. Throughout the dunes are Maori middens, with layers of shell and other reminders of early occupation. The remoteness and length of this beach (left) bring it a unique and awesome quality. From any viewpoint, it disappears into infinity, the sandhills on one side and the long receding stretch of white breakers on the other. This is a wonderful place to surf and swim, to picnic, fish, or collect tuatuas. Annual competitions for line fishermen are held here, drawing large crowds and offering worthwhile prizes. The beach is also a perfect venue for land yacht races held each year.

Pukenui (big hill) is a quaint village on the shore of Houhora Harbour and in the past, when the sea was the highway, it was an important link with the south. Commercial fishing companies operate from the wharf (right). Across the water is the hump of land Captain Cook named Mount Camel as it reminded him of a camel lying down on what he called "the desart (sic) shore". Some know the village as Houhora, but this is the name of the wider area within which Pukenui is situated. Tucked away amongst the trees to the shore is the picturesque old Subritzky home built of lath and plaster by a proud Polish family who arrived in New Zealand in 1843 and ran a small fleet of ships and also dealt in kauri gum. Nestling in its grounds is this small building (above top). The Subritzky estate was bought by Subritzky-Wagener descendants and the old home restored. It is open to the public. Alongside it is the famous Wagener Museum (above bottom). Mr Wilf Wagener, a member of a large Far North family, established this remarkable and diverse museum which houses babies' cradles, Maori artefacts, china, typewriters, everything imaginable. Outside are ancient buggies and at times a bullock team. Family members are there playing a pianola, demonstrating washing machines etc, while under the same roof is a pleasant restaurant.

Many large areas of pine planting can be seen throughout Northland, especially on steep country. This view (right) is of a plantation north of Kerikeri. On the slender Aupouri Peninsula running north of Kaitaia to Cape Reinga 35,000 hectares of land have been planted in exotic forest, predominantly pinus radiata. The trees are owned by four companies, one based in Kaitaia specialising in producing triboard. The strong westerly winds blew sand over hundreds of hectares of land in the Far North and to prevent further loss of grassland, it was decided to develop forestry. This required planting marram grass in the sand dunes to stabilise them, then lupin for nutriment and finally the seedling trees. Te Kao, one of many small settlements on the Aupouri Peninsula (top), is the traditional home of the Te Aupouri tribe, many of whom are adherents of the Ratana faith. The gently sloping farmland has been developed almost totally on sand. North of Te Kao is Parengarenga sandspit covering 1600 hectares of glass sand which is barged to glass-

works. South of the peninsula, Kaitaia (left) is the business centre of the Far North. With a population of around 5,000, the town welcomes visitors in Yugoslav, Maori and English. The Rarawa tribe befriended missionaries who arrived here in 1833 and bought 160 hectares from the local chief. In and around Kaitaia (an abundance of food) many Yugoslavs live, descendants of gumdiggers, some of whom arrived in the area more than 100 years ago.

15

On the Karikari Peninsula to the east of Kaitaia, Matai Bay (above) is one of the gems of the Far North. Here two crescent-shaped beaches are divided by a headland with a small pa site on the summit. The beaches are safe for swimmers, while the bay is popular, too, with fishermen and skin-divers. Several interesting walks can be taken from here. The Department of Conservation has developed a camp with toilets, water and an outside shower. Although some distance from shops, the camp is fully occupied each summer. Waima (left) is a small settlement situated in a valley amid pleasant Hokianga farmland south of Rawene. It is famous for two things. One was its huge oak tree, nurtured from an acorn planted in a pot by Mrs John Warren, a missionary's wife, and taken to Waima in 1831 to flourish until dying comparatively recently. Waima's other claim to fame dates from 1880 when local Maori refused to pay Dog Tax under a new Act and there was almost a war. Roads leading to Waima bring a sense of isolation felt throughout the Hokianga district. This scene, with its rolling farmland and background of native forest is typical of the area.

When the Hokianga Harbour was the highway in times past, many structures in Rawene were built over the water (above). Today buildings in the town are few and quaint and some, like the Methodist Church, the former Wharf Hotel, the lockup and the Masonic Hotel, are historic. Life is a leisurely business on Rawene's waterfront (right). There is time, there, to look out over the water at the mountains beyond, time to sit and think as you watch the clouds roll by, time to pick daisies. However, in the summer, the pace in this quaint little town quickens as holiday-makers gather there. For some time Rawene was known as Herd's Point after Captain Herd bought land on behalf of the first New Zealand Company. It was said that the chief who sold the land was not entitled to do so and when legal tangles followed Captain Herd fled to Australia.

The dining-room at Clendon House (right) is full of beautiful furniture, silverware, glass and china, some of which was brought from Sydney in the 1830s and some from Kent, where James Reddy Clendon was born. Captain Clendon was later to become a colonial magistrate and United States Consul in New Zealand. Now owned by New Zealand Historic Places Trust, his Rawene home, Clendon House (top, far right), is open to the public. Built in the 1860s, it was insured with the New Zealand Insurance Company who described it as "a building covered with shingles, containing eleven rooms comprising dwelling-house, kitchen and schoolroom". A large brick oven for baking bread is mentioned. Today the kitchen shows signs of alteration by many hands over many years. Captain Clendon's second wife, Jane, 40 years his junior, and her son, George Thomas Clendon, were instrumental in preserving the home for the enjoyment of all New Zealanders. Jane's aura of peace and serenity are said to pervade the house. Close to Clendon House the Rawene ferry crosses back and forth between the town and the Narrows near Kohukohu, a trip of ten minutes, (bottom, far right). Accommodating 16 cars, the ferry saves motorists many miles of driving over unsealed roads. Ambulances bring cases across the water to the Rawene Hospital.

The north and south heads of Hokianga Harbour (left) resemble a moonscape. A bold rocky cliff at the south end is surmounted by an old signal station, whereas the north head comprises spectacular moving sand dunes up to 17.5 metres high. Long and narrow, the harbour itself is a ragged tear in Northland's west coast, framed on all sides by forested mountains. Small towns dot its shores, remnants of old kauri milling and gum-digging days. It is to its southern shores that city holiday-makers escape in search of remoteness and peace. Along the harbour shore is the Wesleyan Mission House at Mangungu (below). From when it was begun in 1828, it grew slowly into a "mission house of sorts", only to be burned down in 1838. By mid-1839 the present building was completed and it was here that a second signing of the Treaty of Waitangi took place on February 12, 1840. In 1855, by which time the local population had declined and Mangungu had become a backwater, the house was moved to Onehunga. Later it was moved to another Onehunga location where it stood until being moved back to Mangungu in 1972. The house overlooks a graveyard in which Maori converts are buried along with European settlers, sawyers, seamen and children of missionaries.

In Northland there are long stretches of mangroves which grow in tidal waters (right). At low tide their breathing roots can be seen protruding from the mud. The leaf of the tree has glands which can disperse surplus salt from the water. Because falling leaves provide food for snails, fish and birds, the mangrove is important in our ecological system. This view of Whangaroa shows one of the many spectacular rocky outcrops which are common in the area. The historic Toukahawai meeting house in Omanaia near Rawene (above) sits placidly against a background of hills covered with bush. Omanaia (the place of the manaia) gets its name from the birdlike figure in many Maori wood carvings. Peretane Papahurihia, Hone Heke's chief priest, is buried in the 1884 Methodist graveyard here. After his death as a Christian his previous cult followers, the Nakahi, moved his grave when their prayers proved faulty. Because they prayed under cover of darkness they were known as the Blackouts.

These three buildings are part of the Mangonui Conservation Zone which runs along the village foreshore (over page, bottom right). Closest to the camera is a gift shop known as the Wharf Store, built before the turn of the century. Behind it on a rise is the old Courthouse dating from 1892. The third building is the old post office, built in 1904 and now a restaurant. Mangonui was once the centre for the Mangonui County and when the sea was the highway, it was the busiest northern port. This view (over page, left), taken from Rangikapiti pa, looks down on Mangonui Harbour and also on little Mill Bay, where a large timber mill once stood. Now the bay is a safe haven for pleasure craft. Mangonui is the base for commercial fishermen who work Doubtless Bay and beyond and use the fine facilities provided for them on the wharf (over page, top right), including the ice plant installed by Moana Pacific Fisheries. The plant can hold 18 tonnes of ice. When they are in port, working boats can be seen riding at anchor amongst yachts and launches. The wharf is a popular place for both adults and children, especially in the school holidays (over page, centre right). Even "kingies" can be caught here.

The gentle character of Coopers Beach (right) in Doubtless Bay makes swimming safe for all ages, while it attracts diverse pleasure craft, surf skiers, kayakers and the like. There is an excellent shopping centre at the beach, including a dive shop, and on the foreshore adjoining it is one of the finest camping grounds in the country. Pohutukawa trees provide welcome shade in the heat of the summer. Every inch of the highway from Auckland to Coopers Beach is sealed and from the road it is possible to step on to the silvery sand. The name derives from the days when whaling ships came into Mangonui Harbour for food and water. It was at Coopers Beach nearby that the ships' coopers made and mended their barrels. Mount Taratara (above), a rocky volcanic outcrop south of Coopers Beach, is the subject of countless landscape paintings. From the summit the panoramic view includes Whangaroa Harbour to the south and Karikari Peninsula and Doubtless Bay to the north. The mountain's contours differ vastly depending on whether seen from State Highway 10 or from the winding country road arcing around it. Legend tells us that Taratara was a young god who had two wives. When Maungataniwha, a wifeless god, pleaded for one of Taratara's wives, he was turned down and in a fury he knocked off Taratara's head. Seeing her two friends arguing, another mountain, Maunganimi, wept, her tears being the inlets and streams around Whangaroa Harbour.

On the south shore of Whangaroa Harbour (left) is Whangaroa itself, and on the north shore, quaint little Totara North, once famous for its ship-building yards. Whangaroa Harbour is one of the most natural in New Zealand and deep and large enough to accommodate a navy. The heads measure less than 200 metres at their narrowest. From outside the harbour Stephenson's Island blocks them from view. During the last war the heads were mined and an anti-submarine boom built across them. Within the harbour are several islands and also what are known as "mushroom rocks" and "haystack rocks", titles that are self-explanatory. The harbour shores are indented by several beautiful bays haunted by boaties, and reached only by launch is the Kingfisher Lodge, which provides meals and accommodation. On each side of the harbour are lofty outcrops, the most spectacular, perhaps, being the craggy Duke's Nose and St Paul's. It was in this harbour that the unfortunate burning of the *Boyd* took place in 1809. A short distance from the Whangaroa road towards the east coast is Ota Point (above). Even many Northlanders have not seen this fascinating little spot which is tucked away one kilometre from a sealed road. Around twelve homes are gathered together in a tranquil setting by the water's edge on an arm of the Whangaroa Harbour.

Tauranga Bay (above), just south of Whangaroa (long harbour), is the first of a series of breathtakingly beautiful bays on the east coast. Here there is a camp and a store, and on a hillside above Butterfly Bay adjoining it, are pohutukawas to which Monarch butterflies return year after year. Typical of most beaches along this shoreline, Tauranga Bay is kindly and safe. The road to it from the north branches off the Whangaroa road which is sealed, winding along a waterfront edged with mangrove trees to begin with, then opening up to an expansive view across the harbour. An oyster farm has been developed just before the village is reached. The centre of Whangaroa (left) is the Marlin Hotel with the fine Yacht Club headquarters opposite, launches of all sizes anchored close to the shore and seagulls waiting for visitors to provide them with a meal. On the steep hillside behind the village the huge outcrop of St Paul's dominates the skyline. Historic buildings cling to the slopes, amongst them a tiny church and an old post office. Whangaroa is a Mecca for deep-sea fishermen, with a number of charter-boats available for hire. Harbour cruises are an unforgettable experience, especially as they are accompanied by an excellent commentary.

Puketi Forest (bottom left) gives visitors the opportunity of seeing the magnificence of the mighty kauri on the east coast of Northland. A lovely loop drive can be taken by leaving S.H.10 just south of Kaeo and returning to it just north of Kerikeri, or in reverse. The road is not sealed, but the diversion is worthwhile, especially as it is possible to see part of an old timbermill dam en route. In Puketi Forest there are several huge old specimens of kauri, the path leading to them is short and well paved, and trees other than the kauri are labelled for identification purposes. Standing on a spacious platform listening to the silence of the bush and to the bird calls is somehow humbling.

Other lovely bush can be seen when travelling over the Mangamuka Range south of Kaitaia. The Mangamuka River winds through a long valley, the road high above it passing through untouched native bush for many miles (top left). At the top of the Mangamukas is a viewing spot and there are also soda pools. Below the road is an extensive picnic area amid great beauty. Dairy herds are a common sight throughout Northland. In the long dry summers herds can be seen grazing the "long acre" on the roadside, kept off the road by an electric fence. The herd (above) grazes with Mount Taratara towering behind it.

35

Matauri Bay (above) is undoubtedly the most beautiful of a series of bays on an unforgettable east coast scenic drive. The panorama from the road high above it is known as the million dollar view, out to sea and over and beyond the Cavalli Islands. Overseas travellers use reel upon reel of film in the area. Most of the road off S.H.10 is unsealed, but taking it is rewarding. From the hilltop above Matauri Bay the road to the beach is steep and winding, but short. The sand glistens. The remoteness is complete. At the northern end of the beach is a small store and a camping ground and around a corner, there is another beach, small and heavily shingled. Matauri Bay is where Samuel Marsden the missionary first set foot in New Zealand, a plaque at the southern end of the beach marking the reputed spot. And at the northern end is a memorial to the *Rainbow Warrior* which was sunk here after its tragic bombing in Auckland. Just north of Matauri Bay is the sweeping curve of Wainui Bay (right), another gem, with huge pohutukawas which are missing from Matauri Bay. A tiny school below the road has, perhaps, the most wonderful view of any school in the country. There is a small cluster of houses here—otherwise nothing but the endless sea. And peace.

Tapeka Point (right) was kept a secret for many years by those who live in nearby Russell. Only when a subdivision was opened up comparatively recently did others find their way there. The beach has all bathers could wish for—the sea, almost too lazy to lap, the clean silvery sand, grass to lie on if that is preferable and the not-to-be-forgotten view. From Russell itself the tall ship, the *R. Tucker Thompson* (above), takes chartered cruises to sea during the summer months, and who does not thrill at the sight of such wind-filled sails? On board there is a special atmosphere of bygone days, an air of romance on a ship built in the style of schooners sailing our oceans a century ago. The *R. Tucker Thompson* took part in the Australian Bi-centennial First Fleet voyage and has circumnavigated the world. On board, holiday-makers can help with sails, take the helm, listen to stories as tall as the ship itself, or simply laze on deck.

38

The Bay of Islands is somewhere anyone can fish with success. Charter-boat owners take visitors to their special known spots, but private boat owners are knowledgeable too and the fish are there for the taking. Close to rocky islands such as these at Whale Rock (below) there is plenty of snapper, trevally and pink maomao, and birds tell where schools of kahawai are feeding. There is skipjack tuna, too, and perhaps a "kingy". Almost certainly something large or small will be on the line. Light tackle trips are available and short and long trips after big game fish are an option. Based at Paihia, Fuller's luxury catamaran, Tiger III, can travel at high speed. The route taken by the Hole in the Rock cruise (left) passes through game fishing waters to Cape Brett lighthouse, then on to Motukokako Island before reaching Piercy Rock, which was named by Captain Cook after Sir Piercy Brett of the British Admiralty. The Maori name for the rock means "island of the blue-wattle crow". The sheer sides of the rock reach 150 metres and the hole seems too narrow for the catamaran to pass through, but with perfect safety it does. The high domed ceiling reverberates as the vessel ploughs through it majestically and passes out into the sunlight.

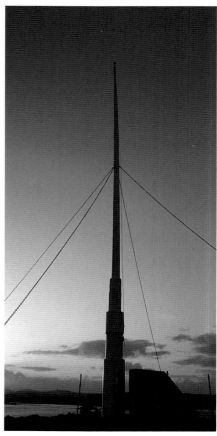

Russell waterfront (far right) is superbly beautiful. No buildings other than the wharf have been erected along the water's edge, but looking out across the water are historic buildings including the Police Station and the Duke of Marlborough Hotel, and Pompallier House which is owned by New Zealand Historic Places Trust. All other foreshore buildings, whether shops or houses, are maintained in historic character, which gives the village a charm of its own. Once known as Kororareka, in early days Russell was dubbed the "hellhole of the Pacific" as a result of the influence of whalers. Ferries ply constantly between the town and Paihia for foot traffic, and for vehicles, between Russell and Opua. The pohutukawas along Russell's grassed shoreline (above) add softness to an already soft scene as dinghies lie peacefully in the shade of their branches. Silhouetted against the sky at sunset, the Russell flagstaff (right) is a reminder that Hone Heke cut down its four predecessors, which led to the sacking of Kororareka in 1845 and the battle at Ruapekapeka. A panoramic view from the 90-metre hill extends to Paihia, Opua and Waitangi, taking in several islands and the Purerua Peninsula. For day-trippers the walk to the flagstaff is well-marked and comparatively short.

SACRED to the MEMORY
OF
COLR SGT. J. M°CARTHY R.M.L.I. AGE 33
PRIVATE ALEX MAY 26
W. LOVELL   SEAMAN - 24
W. LOVE 26
WHITAR DENBY 34
FREDRICK GEO. MINIKIN 23
LATE OF
H.M.S. HAZARD
WHO FELL IN THE DEFENCE OF KORORAREKA
11ᵀᴴ MARCH 1845

Matauwhi Bay (right) has been called Russell's back door. Horse races were once held on the flat area above the beach. As in all other sheltered coves, Matauwhi Bay is a haven for boat owners. In 1835 Christ Church (above) was built in what was Kororareka, now Russell. It is the oldest church standing in New Zealand. Funds for the building were raised by settlers and Charles Darwin also contributed when on a visit to the town. Local Maori gifted the land on which the church stands, with the proviso that both Maori and European had equal rights of burial in the graveyard. The scars left on the walls by cannon balls and musket shells during the sacking of the village in 1845 can be seen today.

There is never a time when there are not sails on the waters of the Bay of Islands (above). Perhaps the presence of all the islands makes sailing more. exciting. Boats can be chartered and tuition given to beginners. Large charter-boats provide snorkels, fins, fishing gear, even bedding, and the skippers all know exactly where the best fishing spots are. Boat owners will find good ramps throughout the bay, and there are Yacht or Cruising Clubs at Opua and Russell and at Doves Bay near Kerikeri. Zane Grey made the Bay of Island's deep-sea fishing famous in the 1920s when he gave the name "Anglers' Eldorado" to the area. Otehei Bay on Urupukapuka Island (left) was his base. Perhaps his influence is the reason the waters around the island are favoured today by deep-sea fisherman. A great deal of early Maori occupation is in evidence throughout the island— ditches and terraces, a living pa site on a headland, an inland pa, kumara pits, and signs of a marae in the centre. There are several archaeological walks on the island, one of five hours, the others shorter.

47

The BAY OF ISLANDS
SWORDFISH CLUB-NZ
DATE 7-2-93
ANGLER BRIAN BETTS
FISH S/MARLIN
WEIGHT 87.8 KGS
TACKLE 24 KG.B/S
LAUNCH ALI BABA
SKIPPER GARY COLES

Long before Kelly Tarlton developed his Underwater World in Auckland, he opened his Shipwreck Museum at Waitangi, near Paihia (right). Kelly was an ex-post office technician but his hobbies were underwater photography and diving. Over the years he had gathered relics from wrecks and needed somewhere to house them. He bought the *Tui*, a former Chelsea sugar lighter which had been used by an Opua potter, had it towed to Waitangi and redesigned its hold. Salvaged items from the *Niagara*, the *Boyd* and the *Wahine* are displayed along with the Rothschild jewellery Kelly suctioned from the ocean-bed near Mahia Peninsula. Visitors to the Bay of Islands can join the

Bay of Islands Swordfish Club at Russell or Paihia for as short a time as a day. The weighing-in of a sizeable catch such as this marlin (left) always attracts a crowd of spectators. Great excitement is aroused on the "wetting of the baby's head". The Paihia waterfront (above) is a bustling spot, especially around the wharf, with ferries coming and going constantly and people of all nations walking and talking, sitting and eating. Opposite is an attractive shopping area and a large carpark where visitors can leave their vehicles for as long as they like with perfect safety. The view over the water is incomparable, beyond the small inner islands to those disappearing into the distance.

James Busby, New Zealand's first British Resident, lived in what is now known as Waitangi Treaty House (far left) from its completion in 1834 until his departure for Australia in 1871. The frame was prefabricated in Sydney. After many alterations and additions, today the house is a fine example of Georgian simplicity. Lord Bledisloe, then Governor-General of New Zealand, purchased the house and the estate around it in 1932 and he and Lady Bledisloe presented it to the nation. The reserve is now administered by the Waitangi National Trust Board. The signing of the Treaty of Waitangi is commemorated on the expansive lawn between the Treaty House and the sea, and every year the New Zealand Navy plays its part (top left). When ships standing offshore are lit up after dark they bring a gasp from the dignitaries and others gathered together. Nowhere can a more fierce haka be witnessed than here, as the signing of the Treaty is remembered (left centre). The largest Maori war canoe, Ngatokimatawhaorua (bottom left), is housed at Waitangi. It carries a crew of 90 and is a magnificent and impressive sight on the water.

There are two approaches to the Waitangi Treaty House (above). This view is from an entrance leading down the side of the house past well-tended gardens. Begun in 1833, the original house comprised a large entrance hall, a dining-sitting room, a large and small bedroom and a dressing room. By the time the Treaty of Waitangi was signed two tiny bedrooms and a storeroom had been added, further additions being made in 1841 and 1870. It was not until the late 1870s that the house was finally completed to its present form. On each side of the Treaty House pohutukawa trees have been planted, with plaques alongside. They are in honour of dignitaries of one sort of another. On the same grounds is this fine Meeting House or Whare Runanga (above top) representing all tribes, a concept of Sir Apirana Ngata. The building opened on February 6, 1940. Outside carvings represent portions of the body of a notable tribal ancestor. Inside are 14 pairs of poupou or wall slabs, each pair representing a different tribe. The woven tukutuku panels on the walls demonstrate a variety of patterns. Overall, both the concept and the workmanship are a triumph for Maoridom. Close to the Treaty House is the start of the Mangrove Walkway (right). Much of it consists of a boardwalk. At high tide fish can be seen and at low tide the breathing roots, mud crabs, mud whelks and the clicking snapping shrimp.

Built for Reverend John Butler in 1820–21, Kemp House in Kerikeri (below) is the oldest wooden house in New Zealand. On the departure of the missionary, the Kemp family purchased the property and occupied the house from 1832 until gifting it to the nation in 1971. Misses Charlotte and Gertrude Kemp lit a lamp in the window to welcome those travelling up the Kerikeri River. New Zealand Historic Places Trust now administers the property. Rainbow Falls (left) are a short distance along Waipapa Road, about two kilometres from Kerikeri township. The parking area is attractive, with large lawns and a grove of puriri trees. Well-maintained paths lead to a wooden viewing platform. When the sun is shining from the right direction, the colours of the rainbow can be seen in the tumbling waters. Beneath an overhanging rock shelf is a cave, inhabited, legend tells us, by a taniwha or river monster. An interesting walking track has been formed between the falls and the Stone Shore bridge.

Kerikeri (bottom, far right) has been called "The fruit bowl of New Zealand". Its Maori history was followed by the arrival of Church Missionary Society members, but a new wave of occupation took place much later when retired tea growers and others arrived from overseas and established orchards. The entire area covered by Kerikeri is flat and small arms of occupation reach out on both sides of what is known as the Kerikeri Basin. The shopping section (top, far right) is small but tasteful, with a character all its own. Because residents cherish trees, there is a special softness even close to the shopping centre which never stops bustling. In this sheltered little inlet at Te Rawhiti near Russell is a camp on the old school grounds (right). The headlands give a sense of protection and the view out to islands in the open sea make all cameras click. The beach here is safe and the water calm and inviting.

Kerikeri Basin (over page) is an oasis where many locals and interesting visitors anchor their craft. The historic Kemp House and Stone Shore look down on the scene which is always placid, with the softness of surrounding trees and their reflections adding to what is already beautiful.

The Mission House at Waimate North (left) is the second oldest surviving building in New Zealand. A portion was erected by the Church Missionary Society in 1831 but the project was not completed for several years. When Bishop Selwyn ran a school at the Station, three such houses stood on the property. However, on the withdrawal of the Maori after the death of a girl, British troops occupied the buildings, burning some and almost ruining this house. Taken over by New Zealand Historic Places Trust in 1959, the building has been restored and is open to the public. The Opua vehicular ferry (bottom right) runs a shuttle service between Opua which is 15 minutes' drive from Paihia, to Okiato, ten minutes' drive from Russell. It crosses the bay every ten minutes, times varying on weekdays and weekends. This obviates an arduous and long drive over unsealed roads. Opito Bay (top right) is the last of several bays on a peninsula reaching out between the Kerikeri and Te Puna (on some maps Mangonui) Inlets. By road, it is quite a distance from Kerikeri on an unmetalled surface. Permanent and holiday homes are grouped together by the shingly beach whose charm lies in its shelter. A boatie's paradise, it is also close to good fishing grounds. Next to it is Dove's Bay, headquarters for the Kerikeri Cruising Club.

Between Whangarei and Kaitaia, a distance of approximately 100 kilometres each way, Kaikohe (above) is a supply town serving a large rural area. With a population of around 4,000, it began to grow when the railway reached it. On the summit of the Kaikohe Hill a monument stands to a descendant of Hone Heke who cut down the flagstaff at Russell. The descendant, another Hone Heke, became a Member of Parliament and was highly esteemed by both Maori and European. In between parallel lines of shelter belts at Kerikeri (right) row upon row of fruit trees can be seen, primarily citrus and kiwifruit. Some orchardists have their own packing sheds and employ a number of casual workers in the picking season. Inland from Paihia, Kawakawa is famous for its railway line running the length of the main street. The vintage steam train (above top) is a legacy from the old coal-mining days. Some years ago a company took it over and during the summer months runs three trips daily to and from Opua. In the off-peak months, it runs two trips daily. The journey takes 45 minutes each way and is full of interest, as the train passes through mangroves and a tunnel on its way.

From the highway through Waipoua Forest on the west coast, a walk of 15 minutes brings you to Te Matua Ngahere (right), the second biggest tree in New Zealand, the largest being Tane Mahuta, also in the Waipoua Forest. Te Matua Ngahere (Father of the Forest) is 30 metres in height and has a girth of 16.4 metres. The distance to the first branch is seven metres. The tree stands amongst other kauri which seem slender beside it. In the forest, too, is Maxwell Cottage (above). James Maxwell was Waipoua Forest's first caretaker and lived in this cottage from 1890 until 1920. The roof of the house is shingled with kauri and the paling walls are split kauri. A most interesting museum is housed in the building today, with items from the milling and gum-digging days well displayed. The cottage is within Forest Headquarters which is two kilometres off the highway along a narrow, winding road to spacious lawns and picnic tables.

Visitors can tell when they are approaching Dargaville by the kumara signs along the roadside (left). The town has been called the kumara centre of New Zealand. The kumara or sweet potato (Ipomoea batatas) was much loved by pre-European Maori and is reputed to have been brought here from Hawaiiki by the Tainui canoe. The Maori stored the kumara by burying them in pits. In the harvest season teams of temporary workers can be seen working in the kumara fields all around Dargaville (above) which is situated on the western bank of the Wairoa River, approximately 60 kilometres north of the entrance to the mighty Kaipara Harbour. In early European days it was purely a timber and gum-digging town. Because many diggers were Yugoslavs, today the town welcomes visitors in English, Yugoslav and Maori. Rural activities in the area include sheep, dairy and cattle farming and market gardening. In the town itself there is some light industry. Less than 40 kilometres north of Dargaville are the Kai Iwi Lakes in the Taharoa Domain. Taharoa Lake (far left) is one of three lakes within the Domain. There are five access lanes to the lake, whose rules preclude small craft from exceeding five knots within 100 metres of the shore unless in defined areas. This popular recreation reserve covers an area of 538 hectares.

The Kaipara Heads lighthouse (bottom right) is slightly less than 70 kilometres south of Dargaville, situated on an outcrop of sandstone 278 feet above sea level on the Poutu Peninsula. Built in 1884, it first operated on December 1 that year. Small cottages were built nearby to accommodate the lighthouse keepers. The lighthouse was switched to automation in 1947. The little Pioneer Church at Matakohe (top right) is close to the well-known Otamatea Kauri and Pioneer Kauri Museum south-west of Whangarei. This was the first building in Matakohe. Non-denominational, it was built by settlers in 1867 and for some time was also used as a school and meeting place. It was moved to its present site in 1950, a flagpole marking its original site. The Otamatea Kauri and Pioneer Museum (far right) was built as a tribute to the pioneers of the area. As its name suggests, it is devoted to the kauri and its by-product, kauri gum. Old machinery is there, a colonial cottage, a room containing beautiful kauri furniture, a section displaying all types of kauri gum and articles made from it, another room of photographs of timber-milling days, an excellent shop and a lot more. The models throughout the museum are replicas of those who are or were part of the history of the area. The entrance ticket enables visitors to come and go all day.

Maungatapere is a small settlement slightly west of Whangarei. On fertile volcanic land dairy farms such as this (left) are a common sight, high-class herds featuring throughout the countryside. Horticulture is also an important industry in the area, which is known for its kiwifruit, tamarillos and avocados. Stone walls, a legacy of volcanic activity, are a feature of the landscape. Further west, around Tangiteroria near Dargaville, goat farming (above) was introduced but the economic decline saw all but one milking herd disappear from the area. Dairy, beef and sheep farming are the mainstays of the district.

71

The Whangarei Oil Refinery (above) is a huge and impressive sight. It commenced operations in 1964, producing a range of petroleum products for five New Zealand oil marketing companies. Each refining step involves a separation, a conversion and a purification. End products are motor gasoline, premium kerosene, diesel fuel, fuel oil and bitumen. Eleven thousand tonnes of structural steel, 600,000 metres of piping and 550,000 metres of cable were used in the refinery's construction when it was built on an area of 120 hectares. A scale model at the Visitors' Centre is awe-inspiring. The Whangarei Marina (right) is only a step from the centre of the city and provides a safe haven for yachts. Attractive to photographers and artists is the sea of masts, while lunchtime city workers share the jetties with boat owners and seagulls.

Whangarei (over page) has a population of around 40,000 and is Northland's only city. Nestling in a valley on the banks of the Hatea River, it spreads far and wide over an extensive area. The town's prosperity lies in its deep-water harbour and its three ports—Port Whangarei itself, Marsden Point ten kilometres to the south-east, and Portland ten kilometres south.

Stone walls (bottom left) such as these just outside Whangarei's city boundary at Glenbervie are a feature of many parts of Northland, a legacy of volcanic eruptions. They steal throughout this area and along with the soil, the trees and the gentle countryside, give an air of prosperity to the landscape. A nursery specialising in begonias and gerberas is sited at Glenbervie. Whangarei, too (top left), has an air of prosperity. This is where Northland Base Hospital and Radio Northland are based. A variety of parks and reserves dot the suburbs and the inner city, giving it a feeling of kindliness. Whangarei is the home of the unique Clapham Clock Museum and not least, its Forum North houses the City Council offices and also the Capitaine Boungainville Theatre which seats just under 400. The theatre is named after the ship which burned off Whangarei coast in 1975, salvage money providing some of the cost of the building in which regular lunchtime concerts take place and where there is a fine restaurant. Along the Whangarei Heads road are several attractive beaches, ideal for windsurfing yet close to the city (above). Mount Manaia (430 metres) glowers in the background in this scene.

One of the love-
liest and leafiest places in Whangarei is
Mair Park (right), situated on the banks
of the Hatea River and within walking
distance of the city centre. The original
park of around three hectares was a
New Year gift to the city by the late
Robert Mair. Stepping stones once used
to cross the river have been replaced by
a bridge connecting this park to the
equally bushclad Dobbies and Drum-
mond Parks. Throughout the parks is a
network of beautiful walks, some easy,
some difficult. The William Jones
Camping Ground adjoins Mair Park.
Whangarei Falls (above) are popular
with visitors and locals alike. Only six
kilometres from the city, they have a
drop of 25 metres. In the river are
several natural swimming holes and the
bush walks in the vicinity are easy. The
Rotary Club linked two areas of superb
bush with a Bridge of Friendship from
which the view of the falls is spectacular. The picnic area at the falls is a
favourite with city dwellers.

One of the most beautiful small beaches near Whangarei is Whale Bay (below), hiding at the foot of a peninsula just north of Matapouri. From a carpark a track through delightful bush brings you to the shoreline which is clean and lined with pohutukawas. The walk takes approximately ten minutes and although steep in parts, is reasonable if you are fit. Pahi Bay (left) is also a hideout for those who like seclusion and is yet another of Northland's superb and safe beaches. South of the Whangamumu Peninsula, it is almost two kilometres in length, with two pa sites at the southern end. Boaties enjoy a visit to this quiet little gem.

The farming scene at Whananaki (left) on the east coast north of Whangarei is repeated through Northland, where kindly farmers allow friends to spend summer holidays in havens with safe beaches and fine fishing. North and South Whananaki are connected by a long footbridge. Another lovely east coast beach is at Oakura (above), south of the Bay of Islands. The sea all along this coast brings fishermen, divers and boaties to it in the summer season. At the northern end of the beach is a ski lane. At Oakura there is a boat ramp and a store, and motels and a camping ground.

All around the Tutukaka Heads (below) pohutukawas grow profusely, a magnificent sight at Christmas time. Although water sports enthusiasts come here in their hundreds there is always plenty of room because the Tutukaka Coast as it is known stretches for 18 kilometres and within it are a dozen beautiful beaches. Divers especially love the area, particularly from January to May, when they can see most that is offering in sub-tropical waters. At the little haven of Tutukaka (the kaka perch) itself (right) facilities include a Game Fishing Club, a motor-camp, a licensed hotel and motels.

Langs Beach (right) is 12 kilometres south of Waipu and is typical of Northland's east coast beaches. Visitors are attracted to it for its swimming, surfing and rock fishing. The village is tiny, with a cluster of residential and holiday homes. Further north is Whangamumu Bay (left), as far as you can get east of Russell. The road is not inviting but the journey worth it. The Whangamumu peninsula is now a reserve with walks over it and spectacular views. The harbour is famous for its history of whaling. The three Cook brothers established a shore station north of Whangamumu before moving to

Whangamumu itself and employing an unheard-of method of whaling. A net with a large mesh was suspended between the mainland and a certain rock, and after being caught, the whales were speared and brought ashore. By 1924 the business was firmly established but closed down in the late 1930s when prices for whale oil declined. A few crumbling concrete ruins are all that remain of the unusual venture. Further south, near Whananaki, is Otamure Bay (above) with its motor camp and good fishing and swimming. As at other east coast bays, the sunrises here are also memorable.

A number of holiday homes of Aucklanders are dotted amongst those of permanent residents at Mangawhai Heads (above), a pretty, sheltered and secluded spot away from the hustle and bustle of the city. Close by at Mangawhai itself is a shopping centre. To the north Langs Beach (left) offers lazy holidays and seclusion too, and a lovely long view of Waipu Heads.

Mansion House on Kawau Island (right) was the home of Sir George Grey, twice Governor of New Zealand. Purchasing the island in 1862, he converted the copper mine manager's house into the imposing Mansion House of today. To the native bush he added exotic shrubs and trees from sub-tropical countries all over the world. He also acclimatised fruits and at great expense imported animals and birds of his choice to complete his "earthly paradise". After Sir George sold the island in 1888, Mansion House became a guest-house for visiting yachtsmen and others. Now it is closed to visitors. The island has been sub-divided and is a holiday haven for many.

Before copper was discovered on Kawau Island (above) manganese had already been found. Conflicting dates are given for the discovery of copper for which rights were obtained only to the high-water mark. A second mine was established between high and low tide marks by another company and there was a legal battle until the two companies were amalgamated. Over a four year period copper worth sixty thousand pounds was mined before the mine closure in 1869. Drilling in the 1930s failed to find a workable lode.

On an eastern inner reach of the Kaipara Harbour the Minniesdale Chapel (above) sits in solitary splendour. It was built in 1867 for the remnants of a party of English colonists who arrived in the area in 1862–1863. The group formed the Albertland Christian Colonisation Movement, named for Prince Albert, Queen Victoria's Consort. The quality of the land allotted to them was disappointing, communications were virtually nil and dissension grew amongst the settlers themselves until most left for elsewhere. Those who remained worship in this tiny church. Omaha Bay (left) is one of several lovely bays close to Warkworth. The sense of isolation is complete here. A feature of some of the steep farmland is the pleated effect as seen in this photograph.

Orewa Beach (right) is just over three kilometres long and less than an hour's drive north of Auckland on S.H.1. Never anything but bustling, it was once a sleepy small village, but over recent years its popularity has seen it grow into a sizeable town, houses now mushrooming on the hills beyond the seashore. Orewa Beach provides good swimming and fishing. A few kilometres north are the Waiwera Thermal Springs. Thirty kilometres north of Orewa is Warkworth, with a population of less than 2,000. Surrounded by prosperous farms, the picturesque village lies on the banks of the Mahurangi River. In summertime pleasure craft anchor by the wharf which is close to the commercial centre. The Wilson Portland Cement Company established its headquarters on the river bank in 1865, making use of the high-grade limestone in the area. When the company moved elsewhere, its buildings here were abandoned, the remains adding a special character to the town (above). Less than five kilometres distant is New Zealand Post's Satellite Earth Station, covering almost 17 hectares. Access to Kawau Island is from Sandspit near Warkworth.

On the coast 25 kilometres east of Warkworth is the seaside settlement of Leigh, where permanent and holiday homes are gathered together close to the shoreline. The beach is much sought-after and the sealed road to it from Warkworth passes through gently rolling pastoral land (above). Leigh is close enough to Auckland to please city weekenders. Another road to Leigh is from Wellsford, north of Warkworth on S.H.1 and a round trip is pleasant. Approximately 15 kilometres south of Warkworth and only a step off S.H.1 is historic Puhoi, meaning slow water. The tide here only creeps up the river, it is said. In 1863 a group of German-speaking Bohemians from near Prague arrived to take up land grants in the Puhoi area. The soil was so poor that many moved away, but some have remained there ever since, bringing a special character to the minute town. Its most well-known building is the hotel (left), well worth a visit to see the relics and photographs of Puhoi's colourful past on display. For some reason the authorities have had trouble with road-signs at the main highway junction, several having disappeared or been vandalised over the years. This is why the current sign is well above an ordinary ladder's reach.